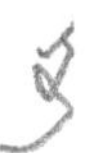

NOSTALGIA'S THREAD

The poems in *Nostalgia's Thread* are an accessible and provocative reconsideration of the American experience as depicted in ten of Rockwell's best-known paintings. These poems remind us that visual art is never static, the beholder's eye never innocent. They bear witness to the fact that each cultural era must reinterpret its rich artistic inheritance within the context of its current collective experience. With unflinching honesty and deep compassion, these poems present a personal and national past which is both comforting and disturbing, both "nostalgia's thread" and "the barbed wire / of memory."

Nostalgia's Thread

Ten Poems on
Norman Rockwell Paintings

Randall R. Freisinger

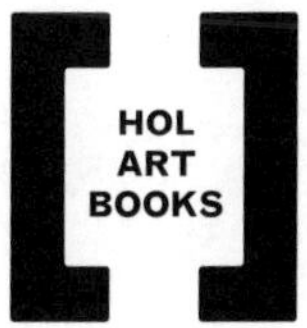

WWW.HOLARTBOOKS.COM

TUCSON, ARIZONA

Printed in the United States of America
on FSC Mixed Sources certified, 30% PCW recycled paper

Project Team:
Randall R. Freisinger, *Author*
Therese Broderick, *Project Manager*
William Trowbridge, *Editor*
Margaret Kimball, *Designer*
Dennis Walikainen, *Publicist*
Alana Nolan, North Wind Books, *Bookstore Sponsor*

For more information about this book, including permissions to reproduce
the text in whole or in part, please e-mail info@holartbooks.com

Library of Congress Control Number: 2009932598

ISBN 978-1-936102-03-7
ISBN 978-1-936102-04-4 (hardcover)
ISBN 978-1-936102-05-1 (ebook bundle)

holartbooks.com
#A-020

For my sons,
Ian and Quentin

Anyone who can handle a needle convincingly can make us see a thread which is not there.

—E. H. Gombrich,
Art and Illusion

[B]elow the surface of even [Rockwell's] most charming children lie the anxieties and fears of the future.

—Thomas Hoving,
"The Great Communicator,"
Norman Rockwell: Pictures for the American People

CONTENTS

<-- -->

The Discovery
(1956)

The kids in Norman Rockwell's America always grow up.
—Dave Hickey,
"The Kids Are All Right: After the Prom"
Norman Rockwell: Pictures for the American People

You stand aghast in your pajamas, just a boy
    of six or seven, your feet cold even on the carpeted floor,
your back turned to your father's dresser, the one
    on top of which each night he places the mysterious
contents of his trouser pockets, the loose change and keys
    and lucky silver dollar and other things you think
might offer clues to the world of work he goes to
    when he leaves the house at dawn five mornings a week.
Just moments ago, you thought that secret
    life might somehow explain this astonishing fact:
your father seems to know Santa and keeps
    in his bottom drawer a change of clothes for him.
It's true you were snooping, despite the chance,
    better than even, you would be caught

and punished by a lash or two of his belt
    or, worse, a week's worth of going without
dessert. But your eyes and mouth
    in their nearly perfect O of recognition move
quickly on to a far more subversive revelation.
    This is a proper place for Act I to end: you turning
to us, your hushed audience, Santa's red cap in your hand,
    and all of us reminded once again as we leave our seats
at intermission for a glass of wine or a cigarette
    that innocence is little more than a brief overture
to the operatic entanglements of loss.

⤛ ⤜

Years later, looking back, you see such deception
    was entirely needed, for it would be theme
and variation for all subsequent acts
    in this show that has run so long, the one
the gods in their role as producers might close
    at any moment. And you've played
every part, from lead to foil to clown,
    and have helped provide a major amount
of the comic relief in this theater
    of the necessarily absurd. But still,
you're grateful for the gift your father never meant
    for you to unwrap so soon, this discovery
that the world is all theatrics and special effects.
    That Christmas Eve morning, the door
stage left stood open, and right on cue he called
    you to breakfast. At the table you carried
it off, suspending your newly acquired disbelief,
    as you did for the days to follow,

and for the year or two beyond. And when
      your parents thought it time for you
to know, your surprise seemed convincing enough.
      Since then you've continued to improvise.
You've continued to rehearse the necessary
      lies upon which a life in the theater
depends. And you have stayed in character
      all these years, even when you've botched
more than your share of the lines.
      Even now, when prop by prop the set topples
nightly all around you, and the curtain, fouled,
      refuses to fall, and the lights on stage
are more and more blinding, what you long for
      most of all is one last graceful exit.

Girl At Mirror
(1954)

The woman had come because her husband wanted
    to kindle memory, to see again the images
he claimed defined him as a boy, images
    that came monthly to his house, resting for weeks
on coffee table and kitchen counter and bathroom
    hamper, images he swore had shaped
his sense of growing up in America.
    She'd studied art in college

and remembered the dismissal and scorn
    her teachers preached for mere illustrations
of The Real. So she had prepared herself
    not to like what people of taste she knew
disdained. Nor did it help that she found,
    in every gallery room, tourists
in striped shirts, white belts, gold chains,

    and tight fitting clothes gushing bloated approval
because, for them, every canvas seemed to contain

a fool's gold nugget of truth imbued with a smile
or a pinch of nostalgic rue, because to them
    beauty meant the world they knew had been reproduced
perfectly in paint. And it was true
    that in the course of an hour the woman found
a great deal to dismiss: rustic rubes

    in antic poses, do-good Boy Scouts and
avuncular barbers and tomboys with black
    eyes and sentimental fêtes for FDR's
Four Freedoms, which she believed in
    the cash nexus of America were mostly sham
anyway. But one painting kept her
    circling back: A girl in a white lace slip

sitting before a mirror, peering quizzically
    at herself, her doll on the floor tipped
over or falling, as if this simple act
    of adolescent self-absorption meant time
for childhood play had suddenly passed.
    At her feet an opened lipstick, a comb, a box
of powdered rouge. On her lap a magazine,
    open to a photo of a Hollywood star

whose glamour seemed impossibly far removed
    from what the girl saw returning her gaze
in the mirror: Those wistful eyes that said
    she had glimpsed something of the transient
nature of beauty, the consequences of time.
    The woman recognized the allusive nod
the canvas made to old masters—Velazquez,

La Tour—whose pensive women gazing
into mirrors documented in paint the very dawning
        of self-consciousness. And because she knew
a painting, no matter how abstract,
        invites its viewers to step inside the frame,
to make the implied story theirs with footage
        from their own lives, it was now she
staring into that mirror, remembering

        how once she, too, in her ugly phase felt farther away
than ever from the swan her parents promised.
        How the inaudible whisper of longing
had grown into a moan for which she could find
        no voice. When she was twelve, she had sat
just like this one night, gazing into the mirror
        of her vanity, just hours after the blood prophesied

by her mother had begun to seep from
        between her thighs while she sat at a movie
with friends. And she remembered how
        a few weeks later, and without her even knowing
it, she found her thoughts orbiting around a boy
        she'd never really noticed, a boy who suddenly
burned in the night sky of her mind
        like a bright and newly discovered planet.

She remembered how his first tight-lipped kiss
        made her want both less and more. How is it possible,
she recalled thinking then—a question that bothers
        her still—to know wrong from right
when both flesh and spirit extemporize

in such eloquent, deceptive tongues?
Now she was startled to feel the hand of her husband, soft,

    stabilizing, on her shoulder, calling her back.
The hand she had seized at first to keep
    her from falling, the hand that had led her
through the loss of their first child, the one that helped
    her unravel the hopeless mare's nest of a placebo
lover, the one a few years later still willing
    to worship in the ruined temple of a vanished breast.
Hand in hand they browsed the gift shop,

    then made their way down the winding path
to the parking lot. It was early
    October, and the Berkshires were in full scale
revolt against the looming absence of color.
    On the drive home, they stopped at a stand
for pumpkins, and as they carried the one
    they had chosen to their car, something about

the slant of the dying sun, the burning hills,
    and the autumnal drumming of her heart
led her to wonder how long life might otherwise
    have seemed, and art longer still, were we not so
much like foolish painters asleep at our easels,
    sure that beauty would patiently hold its pose
and the morning light remain forever.

Girl With Black Eye
(1953)

At twelve, here you are, waiting outside
    the principal's office, one eye closed
and darkening—a shiner of pride,
    your widening smile seems to say.
You've been here before, each time
    for acting like a boy and striking
out at the playground bully with a closed
    fist. He is your steady sparring partner
as you ready yourself for a bout
    with the future, and if you look hard
enough you can already see
    that rigged card of heavyweight
men whose punches and counterpunches
    will take place in a ring circumscribed
by neither ropes nor rules. The kids
    at school, the teachers, even your
own parents have taken to calling
    you "Tomboy," a phase most girls pass
through with no true harm, except for the few
    the grownups claim go on

to defy the rules of nature and shame
    the clearest intentions of God. Here you sit,
your hair askew, beribboned pigtails a mess.
    It's 1953. Your blouse is torn,
your plaid skirt ripped, your knees
    scraped and bandaged. The present
must seem to you elementary enough,
    nearly as simply sketched as the work
of art by one of the school children
    on the wall behind you. Your closing
eye and raw knuckles percuss your blood
    like drums in a call to insurrection.
Listen: Can you hear the whispered worry
    of teachers passing in the hall?
Do you see how the door to your left is ajar,
    as if in your lyric assault on the masculine
world you had pried open the gates
    of power itself? Do you note the concern
on your principal's face? It bears tacit
    witness to past and future.
It says you are anarchy, a disturbing vector
    of will. It says Father can no longer tell
you he knows best. It says you can't
    for much longer be expelled.

Freedom of Speech
(1943)

—Office of War Information, 1942

At the gallery, you watch a man pause
    before one of Rockwell's famous Four Freedoms,
the centerpiece, your rented headphones tell you,
    of this retrospective for and about
the American people. In the frame, a man,
    by appearance common and perhaps unaccustomed
to speaking in public, has risen to his feet
    at a small town meeting to say
what is on his mind to his fellow townspeople
    who have turned their gaze on him with
obvious respect and affection.

And just as a painting invites you to step into
    its frame and complete the story, so do those
who stand before a work of art in still and silent
    witness. The man who has paused,

for example. Because of the time
        of day and his careless choice of clothes, perhaps
he is recently retired. Perhaps he has come
        to a point in his life when he feels invisible
to the rest of the hurly-burly world. You see
        how he wears fatigue like an enlarged heart
on his sleeve, the sleeve he perhaps pressed
        free of wrinkles this very morning
because habit is most of what remains
        of a life once full and busy. Or say his wife
has recently died. For him, then, the painting
        is less about speech than it is about grief,
about the way words have failed to convey
        the pain in that swollen heart on his sleeve.

Perhaps the painting is about the longer and longer
        pauses he suffers as one half-formed sentence
jostles against a nervous herd of others, the way
        interstate traffic at day's end slows and narrows
to a single and inexplicable lane. For him,
        the younger man in the painting who has risen
to speak might just as easily be saying nothing
        at all, his tongue still tangled in the barbed wire
of memory while those waiting to listen
        prompt him with expectant eyes.
You suspect this man in the gallery is thinking
        that, if pictures are worth a thousand words,
then a single word can bear the burden of countless
        pictures. If you were to tap him
on the shoulder, grab his sleeve, ask him to confirm
        your imagined story, he would probably flee.

On the other hand, perhaps it's you with the heart
     on your sleeve, and it's you who really needs
to tell someone—that stranger perhaps—
     what you have come to believe about speech
and its exaggerated freedoms. You might begin
     with that morning long ago when police in riot gear
surrounded you and others protesting
     in front of the Student Union, how they loaded you
into buses from the local schools. You might tell
     this stranger you are now holding by the sleeve
that you were all still children really, taught by home
     and church and state to cultivate a conscience
and trust in freedom to speak freely.

You could tell him you knew other children
     like you had just been murdered on another campus
and that others less like you were dying every day
     in jungles and rice paddies from napalm and fire,
friendly or otherwise, for reasons that no one
     seemed able to explain clearly. You could tell him
you had done your homework, that you knew war,
     like human history itself, was ruled by the law
of inertia, that something moving keeps on
     in an undeviating line unless disturbed
by an outside force. You wanted to be that force,
     so you marched, you carried candles
at vigil after vigil, you chanted and sang, you stood
     in the way of nightsticks and tear gas.
You inflated yourself to the point of bursting
     with righteous sounds and furious rhetoric,
and when your hour of fret and strut had ended
     and you were on your way to be booked

and printed, you and the others found yourselves bound
    suddenly together by a vow of silence as the cop
in front of the bus schooled you in the latest law
    of the land, the sacred right to say nothing.

The Runaway
(1958)

In the restaurant, a man excuses himself
    from his wife, his friends, his rack
of lamb, the drinks that have finally begun
    to plane smooth the day's splintered edges.
In the lavatory, while his lame, diminished
    stream delays its advent, he stares as he has
for years at the framed print hanging
    above the urinal. How many times,
the man wonders, has he pissed brooding
    beneath this same picture? Recalling
its steadfast presence through the deaths
    of two friends, the near collapse of his marriage,
the slow-to-heal estrangement of one
    of three children, he knows this simple
framed image has been one of the few constants
    in a score of persistently shifting years.
That first time he knew whose painting it was
    and he also knew he was not supposed
to like it. Such sentimental looking back
    to a past mostly mythologized, such a varnished

view of America: this is what so galled true
      connoisseurs of beauty. But he was moved
nevertheless, as if a neurosurgeon's probe
      had stumbled upon some uncharted declivity
in his brain, one that contained all his pleasures,
      real or imagined, from childhood.
Now, looking again at the picture's fixed
      moment, the man feels at once both exiled
from and pulled into the story: a towheaded boy
      and a cop sitting together in a diner,
talking, while the cook behind the counter
      leans close, smiling, listening to what
the boy and cop have to say. At the boy's feet,
      what little a runaway needs wrapped in a red
bandanna and tied to a stick. The narrative
      line, the man guesses, is supposed to be clear,
reassuring, but it leaves him feeling vaguely unsettled.
      Most of his life he's dreamed
about running. From family, from friends,
      from the angina-like press of routine
that often wakes him at night and leaves him
      frightened and barely able to breathe.
There in the dark he wonders what of value
      he might fit into a bindle. What destination
would set him free of his own querulous
      soliloquies, his mind's non-stop interrogations?
As a child he had come to the end of books
      that made him want to fade away
from his own constrained life and enter
      plots he knew must continue somewhere after the last
turned page. His bladder empty, he continues
      to stare at the wistful little vignette

in front of him. One voice urges him to go
     back to his wife, his friends, and his now-cold
meal, and a second cajoles him to trade places
     with the boy in the painting, to be young again,
to ride his thumb toward every selfish whim.
     But a third, the one he knows best, asks
the kinds of questions that freeze a failed Romantic
     like him in his tracks, as if he himself
were nothing but a static image captured in paint
     as he stands before this urinal. Would the wedge
of apple pie that must lie on the counter in front
     of the boy taste sweet or bitter? Would the glass
of milk before him be half full and cold, or warm
     and half empty? Would the cop's eyes be distilled
with kindness or shifting and distant?
     Who but himself will miss him if he chooses
to run away? Who but himself will love
     him if he decides to stay?

The Problem We All Live With
(1964)

—After an account by Robert Coles

Thinkin' on it now, so long after,
    that picture still don't tell the whole story,
not even by half. *Look*, the magazine
    called itself, as if it owned the only right seein'
eyes in the world. Well, we looked,
    we sure did. And we saw how innocent
that niggra girl looked in her white dress, white
    socks, white shoes, and that white ribbon
in that pigtail squiggle of hair. And her face,
    so calm and full of righteous purpose. Hell,
I can tell you this much—her eyes was
    buggin' out and shootin' all over the place,
like a high-strung horse that don't want
    to go where it's bein' led. And look there
at what's scribbled behind her on the school
    house wall—*KKK, Nigger*. And look at
that splat of red, blood for sure you say,
    like moments before some poor son of a bitch

black boy been lined up and shot.
     How many folks bother to see that tomato
all busted up at that one marshal's feet?
     You see them headless deputies walking
two front, two back of the girl, all four
     of them so in step you'd think they was marching
with only a dozin' blue sky their witness,
     not a thousand angry folks hurlin' curses,
and, in their hearts, things a whole lot worse.
     You don't see them marshals, their jowly,
strung out faces, their sweat, and you sure
     as hell don't see their big god dam guns!
This picture don't tell you how it was
     that day. Mr. Rockwell wasn't there.
I was. Maybe he saw it on TV, or read
     about it in one of them hoity-toity
New York papers, and someone said
     he should paint a picture about it, him
up there in that fancy Yankee town
     where I'd wager ain't a nigger for miles
around. There's truth, and then
     there's truth. Fact is, people even now
look at that picture and still feel sorry
     for that little girl. Don't no one paint
a picture says, "Look here, there's good white
     folks hereabouts keeps losin' their jobs, they get old
and sick and have no money to pay the doctor."
     Ain't no picture that shows how some big shot
federal judge from up north comes along
     sayin' that what's right and wrong for these good
folks now all gonna be different. Truth to tell,
     it wasn't that girl herself drawed us to that school

to scream out our guts. Pride mostly,
        it was, I guess. Preachers down here say pride
will knock you flat 'less you watch
        your step. They say, let it fester in your belly
like a rusty fishhook you might as well pay
        the Lord Jesus for a one-way ticket straight to Hell.
Maybe. But a man can only take
        so much. And most folks down here
say nothing is all that different,
        even now, forty years later. I guess
Mr. Rockwell, had he the mind to, could paint
        the streets of damnation so sweet we'd all want
to turn roastin' on spits there for a eternity
        or two, tip our hats and say, *Thank you very much.*
I just bet he could. I'd like to see it.

Christmas Homecoming
(1948)

The innocent eye is a myth.

—E. H. Gombrich, *Art and Illusion*

Having watched people leap
    from smoke-choked windows, paper
drift down like uncanny snow,
    who doesn't want to believe the eye once
was innocent, before bitter fruit. Before Eden's
    gates, framed by seraphic flames, slammed shut?
You feel that now, as your own eyes fall
    on today's mail, Christmas catalogs
with covers that say we must buy
    back our blissful ignorance, trump terror
with the martial force of our dollars.
    One right image equals countless
pep talks from the Oval Office. This one,
    for example: a son home from college, right arm
clutching a stack of gaily wrapped packages,
    left hand holding a hastily packed valise.
Mother embraces, Father is proud, smiling,

wreathed in pipe-smell. And so extended
is the rest of the glowing family gathered
        to greet this boy arrived back home
that even Grandma Moses, in an odd instance
        of painterly license, has joined
the jubilee. And though you cannot see
        the young scholar's face, you know
it must be as brightly lit as the festooned
        and luminous tree he could see from the street
as he shuffled at dusk up the freshly shoveled
        sidewalk, his mind exam-bleary and filled
with visions of the girl he has spoken to
        only in letters these many months.
Sweet dreams and sweeter profits: Who better
        to pitch them both to a memory strewn with debris
than this guileless, homeland artist
        from forever-quaint New England,
this artist who said he could never paint
        an evil subject? True, there's scarcely a trace
of evil in this image of domestic happiness.

But as evil, too, so often lies in the beholder's eye,
        why should you be surprised to find yourself
now in the grip of the deadly sin of envy?
        Who wouldn't want to trade places with that boy?
You want to be young again, and clean
        of conscience, returned to the embrace
of a loving family that never truly existed
        and which you mostly now visit
only in fading photos or rote prayers
        at church when the liturgy's script

cues you it is time for the dying to remember
      the dead. You want to recall the vanished home
of childhood without the collateral damage of wrath
      and uneasy laughter. But who can control
the flight plan of memory? Instead,
      it is 1968. You're on the final approach
to an airstrip in Kansas, and the only colors
      you see through the window are the red
of the cross and one green wing, which bucks
      wind and cuts through a sterile wrap
of gauzy clouds. This is your homecoming,
      the one you neither planned nor wanted.
But here you are, on an air ambulance full
      of Midwestern boys, some in flag-draped boxes
stowed in the dark bay below you,
      others, like you, suspended in rows of cots
like bunk beds at a boyhood sleep-over.
      Dead, alive: All have Purple Hearts.
You do not trust your own beating one.
      Even dialed down on morphine and tranquilizers,
you keep your left hand bivouacked over it,
      keeping track of its newly sprung
rhythms. Someone, perhaps a nurse
      with a festive shred left of hope, has trimmed
the aisle with a single string of lights that blink
      out in reds and greens and blues their news
that this is still the season of birth.
      The boy to your right has only half a face
beneath his swaddling mask of bandage.
      Across the aisle, a double amputee.
IV lines maze the cabin's crowded space,

their glass bottles swinging on gimbals
like censers of incense in the turbulence
    through which you now descend.

It's Christmas Eve day, 1968.
    On a sleigh chock full of torn packages,
these sons of America are coming home
    to Kansas, home of Dorothy and Toto.
And home, you remember, is where the Good Witch
    said the heart must always reside.
An hour's ride will bring you home,
    back to old familiar streets, where, you know, no one
will answer the formal persistent knocking
    of a cold military wind, where wreaths nailed
to doors trail red bows, lamb's blood smears,
    a sign that warns the gray and official car
each time it slows to the curb: *Pass By.*

After the Prom
(1957)

> *Within any painting exist assorted options of motion.*
> *Gravity is beaten, death sent packing…*
>   —Stephen Dobyns,
>   "Oh, Immobility, Death's Vast Associate"

You never went to a formal dance with her
        as these two have. You were never young
together, never held each other in the gym the way
        they just did, shyly, stiffly at first, then growing
more and more at ease with the stored voltage
        arcing back and forth between them each time
they touched. You never strolled with her
        down safe, well-lit small town streets to the corner
soda fountain, never posed on stools in your formal clothes
        while the boy working behind the counter leaned
across the thick marble to smell the quiet explosion
        of her white gardenia. And no one
ever envied you both the way that other man does, sitting
        next to them—pilot's jacket, military hat—thinking

perhaps how much of his own innocence he left above
       the earth in flak-infested skies so kids like these could go on
making *tableaux vivants* out of prelapsarian love.

Your life together began with a death—her husband,
       father of two sons, your best friend—and death is always
a beginning. Night after night, at this club
       or that, you neither heard the music nor cared.
Sorrow had a good steady beat, one you could dance
       to, and so you danced, while Grief, that great prig,
paced the dark edges of the floor like a Puritan,
       waving his black flag of decorum that said *Stop:*
Don't go there. Did you kiss that first time
       because you danced? Or did you dance because you kissed?
And later, at the counter in the all-night diner, who
       but Hopper might have seen fit to paint you
facing each other over coffee and hung-over
       desire, stiff in your formal attire of loss and desperation,
the wine still clapping like flamenco dancers in your ears?
       The cook, stippled with sweat and grease, leaned
into you with eggs that stared up from the whites
       of their plates with jaundiced eyes. A kid
with pink spiked hair and dope-inspired grin
       studied star charts on the walls of his brain.
The words you wanted were temporarily out
       of print, on back order, so through the window
you each watched the traffic light at the corner repeat
       its steady late night cautions. *Yellow, yellow,*
yellow, it said: the kind of caution speeding
       bodies are bound by time to ignore.

Rosie the Riveter
(1943)

Mondays it's volleyball with balloons,
    Tuesdays Bingo, Scrabble, Clue, or cards,
Wednesdays reserved for Arts & Crafts.
    Each day is carefully choreographed, and best
avoided, the old woman belicves. If only
    they'd leave her alone in her room,
she could wander without purpose
    the pathless and vacant acreage of her mind
like a child in a fairytale forest, lost,
    unperturbed by those brightly colored birds

following close behind, eating the crumbs
    of bread she drops to find her way back
to her bed and sleep. Today the game
    is Nostalgia, offered several times each week
to jog memory, make it wearable a bit longer,
    like a darned sock or old sweater, mended
each morning of the ragged holes the hungry
    moths of dementia chew at night in secret.

In the activity room, aides play Big Band music
    and videotapes of Pathé newsreels, once

shown—*this* she inexplicably remembers—
    before the main feature in regal and balconied theaters.
The residents view slides of memorabilia
    meant to take them back to days when youth
pulsed strong and true and they were immune
    to the foreshortenings of time. A few
lip synch old familiar tunes by Bing or
    The Andrew Sisters, but most slump
in their chairs, jaws slack, attention fixed
    beyond all human sensing, as if they hear

from afar angelic harmonies or see, approaching
    slowly across a vast expanse of quavering
heat and sand, a long-dead loved one waving
    slow motion, or Death himself coming to claim
a last dance. In her year's residence, only a few times
    has a shard of meaning, suddenly excavated
from her bulldozed past, animated her face
    with pleasure or pain, as one does now,
her gaze galvanized by an image projected
    on the screen— a woman, young, hair red

and cropped, arms bare and muscled
    like a man's, a sandwich in one hand,
a rivet gun at rest in her lap. *Rosie the Riveter*:
    She's seen this picture often, and over the years
it had come to stand for home-front resilience
    in times of war. But the first time, a May

day half a century ago, it arrived in the morning
     mail with two letters carried from wherever
he was, fighting with Ike, trying to stop
     the world's dervish spin into chaos. It was irony

of the kind that sometimes makes the universe seem
     perverse—this magazine cover, his letters, and news,
formal and terse, already sorted for the afternoon's mail,
     news that would make the postman's leather pouch heavy
with grief. She did not open the morning's letters
     at first. Instead, she rocked gently on the front
porch glider and studied this androgynous figure
     at once smug and saintly in her patriotic pose, Old Glory
furling behind her, a halo oddly gracing her head,
     her sturdy shoes resting on the spine of *Mein Kampf*.

The old woman recalls staring at the strange contrast
     between the powder compact and lace hankie wedged
in one pocket and the phallic gun silenced for lunch.
     All of it seemed to say those at home were safe
from Hitler's spreading sickness, that women were
     permitted to be strong in the absence of men,
like Penelope with Odysseus away,
     but they must never forget who they are
once wars are over. Nothing in her life at that moment
     led her to believe she could ever possess such strength

as Rosie conveyed. Not the baby, colicky
     in his upstairs crib, not the nearly empty icebox
and the years of rationed desire, not the bed,
     so long lonely, not the house, with its mortgage

and nightly bombardment of small alarming sounds,
     and certainly not the two letters—whatever
they would fail again to say—that lay nested in her lap,
     letters from the already dead, as she would learn
in the heat of that very day when…when….What?
     As if someone had fooled with the rheostat

of memory, the old woman's face suddenly darkens,
     and, along with it, her past. She sits for a few moments
as though a blank video tape were rewinding
     in her head. *Snack time*, the aides announce
with the kind of artificial cheer she's grown tired of.
     She will have none of it, the saccharine cookies
and sour lemon drink some residents blame
     for the widening gaps in their memory.
No. Slowly she rises up on her walker's worn grips
     and struggles unassisted to her room.

Maybe she will talk for a while on the phone
     to her dead sister, no longer surprised
that calls can come from such long distance.
     Or perhaps she'll take the streetcar downtown to shop,
then stop for a cup of coffee and a piece of pie.
     Instead she sits and stares. Why measure
how long? Her gaze is fixed on the Call Chain
     that hangs within easy reach above her bed.
She has asked over and over what it is.
     Why has no one ever told her? she wonders.

In the near darkness of her shaded
     room, the chain reminds her now of a pretty necklace

a boy once gave her. What was his name?
    She waits. It will not come. So she enters
the woods again. A breeze shakes the bare
    branches that lie like crazed cartography
on the blank page of sky. *Come*, she says
    to the many faceless boys, whose names rise
about her like fallen leaves on a wind blowing
    steadily now, from everywhere, all at once.

Artist Facing Blank Canvas II
(1978)

In agony of soul this cover was done
                         —Norman Rockwell

Death sits for him nightly now, on this ship
    under steady sail, and Rockwell is struggling
to get it right in light that seems always about to fail.
    The problems? How to complicate again the threadbare
subject, find an ordinary moment, one that will
    reveal Death's deeply human side, his comedian's heart.
How to capture the unmistakable charm
    beneath the bony jut of chin, or to render eyes
that grapple his like hooks sunk fast
    in the flesh of the newly drowned? Master
of props, what should Rockwell use? No scythe, no hourglass,
    no skeletal armature beneath a billowing, hooded robe
could infuse the empathy he hopes to evoke.

Up on deck, beyond the rail, the black sea,
    insomniacal, turns and tosses, slapping at the hull's

curved slats. To escape the ache of untouched canvas,
     Rockwell squints through the winding sheets
of mist for signs of an end to this crossing.
     In his mind the pictures of the life he left
behind are already growing gauzy, indistinct,
     as if this thick fog penetrated the wide boulevards
and narrow lanes of memory itself. Outside of time
     now, how odd that he should miss its aggravations—
the clamor of each *Post* cover almost overdue,
     deadlines riving sleep like an upturned hive of angry bees.

He longs for company, someone to help him slip
     the knot of solitude, someone with an eye
trained for pulling small telling stories from the rubble
     of the common and making their point instantly
clear, no need for the posturing mediations of critics
     and connoisseurs. He thinks of Rembrandt,
his lifelong teacher, whose face is even now still clipped
     to his easel, whose spirit labored with him
daily all these years. He thinks too of Vermeer, Delft's
     genius of light, and of Dickens, that other
artist of the people, who captured the world's rictus
     grin in words, whose characters first stirred
his own passion for sketching the faces his eyes'
     mind conjured each night his father read to him
 while the great hall clock pronounced
     each syllable of the hour, the gas lamp hissed, and
he filled page after page with crude pencil portraits:
     Pickwick, the shiny pate of Micawber,
the simple features of Mr. Dick.

Down below, Death still holds
     his pose, forever patient, taking pleasure
in art's brevity, in the length without measure
     of life after breath. Rockwell, his eyes still scanning
the white-capped sea for an end to this passage,
     has decided the canvas must for now stay blank.
He listens to the catechistic sameness of prow
     on wave, of masts groaning to the heft of wind trapped
in cupped sails. A bladed moon scrapes away
     at the fog, yet no dim outline of landfall appears.
Only dull light malingers on the horizon, and questions
     flit like florescent phantoms through his mind.
What tint, what mix of colors might reproduce
     that whorled seethe of sea and sky? When will he know
about his new country—its customs, its weather,
     the chronic moods of its people? How, he wonders,
does color register on a dead man's eye?

ACKNOWLEDGMENTS

My thanks to the Norman Rockwell Museum in Stockbridge, MA, for assisting me in some of the research for this book and for allowing me to stand for hours in a very busy gallery, staring at and taking notes on the *Pictures for the American People* exhibit when it was in Stockbridge in the fall of 2001.

A special thanks also to my collaborative team at Hol Art Books for their constant hard work, good will, and marvelous cooperative spirit: Margaret Kimball (Designer), Alana Nolan (Bookstore Sponsor), Dennis Walikainen (Publicist), William Trowbridge (Editor), Therese Broderick (Project Manager), and Greg Albers (founder and publisher of Hol Art Books).

I am grateful to Michigan Technological University for the sabbatical leave that gave me time to lay the groundwork for this project.

Finally, I am indebted, as always, to my wife, Jill Burkland, for her abiding patience, encouragement, and belief.

ABOUT THE AUTHOR

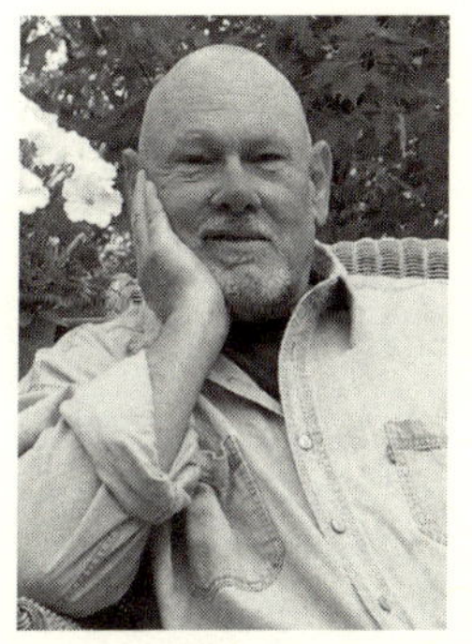

Nostalgia's Thread is Randall R. Freisinger's third chapbook-length collection of poetry. His two previous chapbooks are *Hand Shadows* (Green Tower Press, 1988) and *Running Patterns*, which won the Flume Press Chapbook Award in 1985. His full-length book, *Plato's Breath*, won the May Swenson Poetry Award from Utah State University Press in 1996. His poems have appeared for over forty years in numerous literary magazines and anthologies and have been nominated four times for a Pushcart Prize. He is Professor Emeritus of Rhetoric, Literature, and Creative Writing at Michigan Technological University and lives with his wife, Jill Burkland, on the Keweenaw Peninsula of Upper Michigan.

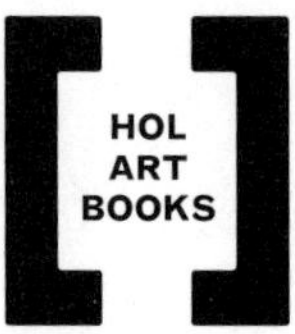

Hol Art Books is an independent press dedicated to publishing and promoting exceptional writing on visual art—classic works of art criticism and history, artist texts and biographies, foreign literature in translation, and the best of contemporary writing.

In a departure from traditional publishing, Hol brings authors and publishing professionals together online to collaboratively identify, evaluate, and develop its titles. This unique model is designed to create a more open and dynamic environment in which to publish books that meet high standards of excellence and have lasting resonance with readers.

Join us.
Visit holartbooks.com to find and publish great books on visual art.